# Genetic Testing: Scientific Background and Nondiscrimination Legislation



Michele Schoonmaker
and
Erin D. Williams



**Novinka Books**
*An imprint of Nova Science Publishers, Inc.*
New York

For permission to use material from this book please contact us:
Telephone 631-231-7269; Fax 631-231-8175
Web Site: http://www.novapublishers.com

**NOTICE TO THE READER**



Library of Congress Cataloging-in-Publication Data:
*Available Upon Request*

ISBN: 1-59454-783-1

*Published by Nova Science Publishers, Inc. New York*

# CONTENTS


| | | |
|---|---|---|
| **Preface** | | **vii** |
| **Chapter 1** | Introduction | **1** |
| **Chapter 2** | Status of Genetic Testing in the United States | **3** |
| **Chapter 3** | Health Information | **15** |
| **Chapter 4** | What Is Genetic Information? | **19** |
| **Chapter 5** | What Evidence Is There That Genetic Discrimination Exists? | **27** |
| **Chapter 6** | How Do S. 306 and H.R. 1227 Compare to Existing Law? | **37** |
| **Chapter 7** | How Would the Proposed Legislation Protect "Genetic Information"? | **39** |
| **Chapter 8** | Title I. Health Insurance | **45** |
| **Chapter 9** | Title II. Employment | **49** |
| **Glossary of Terms and Acronyms** | | **55** |
| **Index** | | **63** |

# PREFACE

Issues surrounding genetic discrimination and privacy in health insurance and employment are currently being debated in the 109th Congress. On February 7, 2005, Senator Snowe introduced S. 306, the Genetic Information Nondiscrimination Act of 2005. The Senate passed S. 306 on February 17, 2005 by a vote of 98-0. On March 10, 2005, Representatives Biggert, Slaughter, Ney, and Eshoo introduced an identical bill, H.R. 1227, in the House. S. 306 is identical to S. 1053 introduced in the 108th Congress, which the Senate passed in 2003 by a vote of 95-0. A House bill, H.R. 1910, did not come to a vote before the conclusion of the 108th Congress. This book provides a comprehensive overview of the status of genetic testing in the United States. The discussion focuses on the key points in the ongoing debate facing the 109th as S. 306 and H.R. 1227 are considered.

S. 306 / H.R. 1227 are supported by consumer groups, the medical profession, researchers, the medical products industry (including pharmaceutical companies), and President Bush, and are opposed primarily by the U.S. Chamber of Commerce. Since the first bills were introduced in the 103rd Congress, many of the arguments and positions supporting and opposing genetic nondiscrimination legislation have remained largely unchanged. Supporters of nondiscrimination legislation feel that current laws are not sufficient to protect individuals from discrimination in health insurance or employment. Further, without protection, individuals are hesitant to seek potentially beneficial genetic services or participate in much needed clinical research. At this stage of debate, opponents believe that current laws provide sufficient protection. They are primarily concerned that new legislation will provide further incentives and additional opportunities for litigation against employers.

Collectively, genetic diseases and common diseases with a genetic component pose a significant public health burden. With completion of the human genome sequence, scientists will now focus on understanding the clinical implications of the sequence information. Clinical genetic tests are becoming available at a rapid rate. Testing is regulated by the federal government and tests are beginning to be included in health insurance benefits packages. Issues surrounding genetic testing and nondiscrimination addressed in this book include:

- What is health information and how is it currently used by health insurers and employers?
- What is genetic information?
- Is genetic information different from other health information?
- What are the implications of having genetic information: for the individual undergoing testing? for his/her family? for society?
- What evidence exists to suggest that discrimination is a problem?
- Will the proposed legislation have been sufficient to protect "genetic information" and "genetic tests" that are of concern?
- How does the proposed legislation compare with existing laws and regulations governing discrimination?

*Chapter 1*

# INTRODUCTION

Issues surrounding genetic discrimination and privacy in health insurance and employment are currently being debated in the $109^{th}$ Congress. On February 7, 2005, Senator Snowe introduced S. 306, the Genetic Information Nondiscrimination Act of 2005. The Senate passed S. 306 on February 17, 2005 by a vote of 98-0. On March 10, 2005, Representatives Biggert, Slaughter, Ney and Eshoo introduced an identical bill, H.R. 1227, in the House.

S. 306 is also identical to S. 1053 introduced in the $108^{th}$ Congress, which passed the Senate on October 14, 2003 by a vote of 95-0.[1] A House bill, H.R. 1910, did not come to a vote in before the conclusion of the $108^{th}$ Congress. S. 306 and H.R. 1227 prohibit health insurance plans from denying enrollment or charging higher premiums to individuals based on the individual's or family member's genetic information. In addition, they contain privacy provisions prohibiting certain uses and disclosures of genetic information as well as prohibiting the collection of genetic information for insurance underwriting purposes. S. 306 and H.R. 1227 also prohibit discrimination in employment because of genetic information and, with certain exceptions, prohibit an employer from requesting, requiring, or purchasing genetic information. If such information is obtained, the bills require that it be treated as part of a confidential medical record. There are detailed provisions on enforcement which generally apply the remedies available in existing civil rights laws such as Title VII of the Civil Rights Act of 1964, 42 U.S.C. § 2000e-4 et seq.

Genetic nondiscrimination legislation has been debated since the $103^{rd}$ Congress.[2] Since that time, many of the arguments and positions supporting and opposing genetic nondiscrimination legislation have remained largely unchanged. President Bush has indicated his support for bipartisan genetic nondiscrimination legislation.[3] Genetic nondiscrimination legislation is supported by consumer groups, the medical profession, researchers and the medical products industry (including pharmaceutical companies). Supporters argue that current laws are not clear on protection from discrimination based on genetic information. Despite the fact that few cases of genetic discrimination can be documented, proponents believe that new legislation is needed to allay the fears of individuals about the potential for discriminatory practices so that they can seek beneficial health services, participate in much-needed clinical research, and otherwise reap the benefits of the publically funded Human Genome Project (HGP). New technologies and applications derived from the HGP will make more information available, and the potential for discrimination more real.

Opposition to genetic nondiscrimination legislation continues to come from some members of the insurance industry and the Genetic Information Nondiscrimination in Employment (GINE) Coalition,[4] which includes the U.S. Chamber of Commerce. The insurance industry argues that current laws are sufficient to protect individuals from discrimination based on genetic information and that additional regulation will be confusing, unnecessary and costly. Insurers argue that it is unfair to prohibit them from acquiring genetic information when they already use other health information. Some groups, such as the American Association of Health Plans, support the premise of federal nondiscrimination legislation and have indicated support for legislation that is consistent with their principles.[5] However, many would further limit the definition of genetic information.[6] One additional bill introduced in the 108th Congress (H.R. 3636) would have prohibited health insurers from discrimination based on *predictive* genetic information but would not have affected employers. The bill had no cosponsors, and many consumer groups indicated that they would not support nondiscrimination legislation without both insurance and employment provisions.

Some employers have questioned whether legislation is necessary because there are few documented cases of discrimination based on genetic information, and there is no evidence that they would use the information if they had it. Randy Johnson, vice president of the Chamber of Commerce's office of labor policy, believes that if the legislation were to pass, it should be narrowed to acknowledge that employers should be able to make employment decisions based on information that some workers with specified genetic markers could pose a "significant risk to others."[7] Other business coalition members believe the definition of "family member" should be revised to include only immediate family.

*Chapter 2*

# STATUS OF GENETIC TESTING IN THE UNITED STATES

## PUBLIC HEALTH SIGNIFICANCE OF GENETIC CONDITIONS

In a traditional sense, individual genetic conditions — usually thought to be congenital syndromes (such as Down syndrome), single gene disorders (such as cystic fibrosis), or metabolic disorders (such as phenylketonuria) — are rare. However, over 15,500 recognized genetic disorders affect 13 million Americans.[8] For example:

- 20 to 30% of infant deaths are attributed to genetic disorders;[9]
- 50% of cases of mental retardation have a genetic basis;[10]
- 15% of all cancers have an inherited susceptibility;[11] and
- 10% of adult chronic diseases (such as heart disease, diabetes, rheumatoid arthritis) have a genetic component.[12]

Today, few effective interventions exist to prevent or cure genetic conditions. The short-term benefits of genetic testing lie largely in the information they provide about risk of future disease and health. The value of genetic information is personal to individuals, who must make medical and other life decisions for themselves and their families. The information can affect decisions about reproduction, the types or amount of health, life, or disability insurance to purchase, or career choices.

Science is only beginning to unlock the complex nature of the interaction between genes and the environment, and their respective contributions to the disease process. Each human being possesses a dozen or so potentially lethal genes[13] —some for recessive disorders that may never manifest but may have implications for offspring, and some for susceptibility to serious illness. Some genes may predispose individuals to certain traits which, though they may not cause disease, could be viewed negatively by society (e.g., low average intelligence, moderately aggressive behavior, mild obesity or chronic conditions). Genetics professionals argue that a better understanding of genetics, and the opportunity to prevent or mitigate unhealthful conditions, necessitates that society accept the full continuum of human biology as part of human variation. This view challenges traditional medical definitions, which tend to characterize health status in discrete terms of "health and disease," "normal and abnormal."

## Human Genome Project Update

The Human Genome Project (HGP) began in 1991. Phase I was an international initiative to decode the entire human genetic sequence. In the United States, the effort was a joint effort of the Department of Health and Human Services (HHS) and the Department of Energy (DOE). The sequence was completed in April of 2003, two years ahead of schedule. The National Human Genome Research Institute (NHGRI) supports genetic and genomic research, investigation into the ethical, legal and social implications surrounding genetics research, and educational outreach activities in genetics and genomics for HHS. In FY2004, NHGRI's budget was $478 million to begin Phase II, which focuses on continuing genomic research to assess the clinical significance of the sequence data.[14]

The Genomes to Life (now called the Genomes: GTL) initiative builds on the DOE's integral role in the HGP. An integrated and predictive understanding of biological systems will enable the United States to develop new technologies related to the detection of biological and chemical agents, energy production, and other DOE statutory missions.[15] The Genomics GTL program began in 2002 and was funded at $18.7 million. In the 108th Congress, S. 682, the Genomes to Life Research and Development Act, would have authorized $100 million funding to the DOE in year 2004, gradually increasing to $455 million in 2008 to continue the work of the program. A similar bill, H.R. 1645, would have specifically established a research, development, and demonstration program in genetics, protein science, and computational biology of microbes and plants to support the energy and environmental mission of the DOE. Neither these bills, nor a more comprehensive bill, H.R. 6, the Energy Policy Act, were passed in the 108$^{th}$ Congress. However, the budget for the program was $63.5 million for FY2004.

# FUNDAMENTAL CONCEPTS IN GENETICS

The following section explains key concepts in genetics that are essential for understanding genetic tests and issues associated with testing that are of interest to Congress.

## Cells Contain Chromosomes

Humans have 23 pairs of chromosomes in the nucleus of most cells in their bodies. Half of the chromosomes are inherited from the mother, half from the father. These include 22 pairs of autosomal chromosomes and one pair of sex chromosomes. Autosomal chromosomes are numbered 1-22 and are the same in males and females. The two sex chromosomes are called X and Y by virtue of their condensed shape.[16] Many syndromes involving abnormal human development result from abnormal numbers of chromosomes (called *aneuploidy)*. The associated conditions or syndromes, such as Down Syndrome, are generally well characterized clinically and easily diagnosed through standard laboratory analysis, such as karyotyping (see Figure 1).[17]

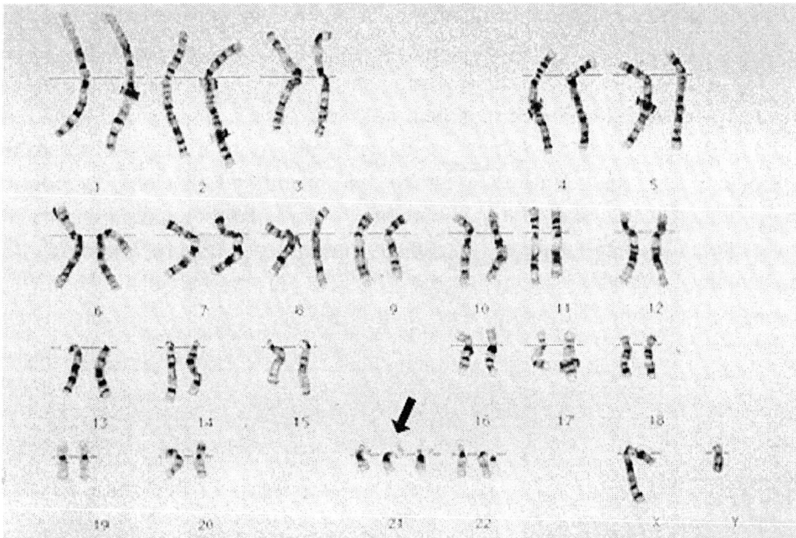

**Figure 1**. A Sample Karyotype from a Down Syndrome Patient

**Source**: [http://medlib.med.utah.edu/WebPath/TUTORIAL/PRENATAL/PREN001.html].

**Figure note**: The karyotype shows 47 chromosomes rather than the normal complement of 46. The presence of the extra chromosome 21, indicated by the arrow, is indicative of Down Syndrome.

Other diseases, such as leukemia, can be caused by breaks and rearrangements of chromosome pieces with other nonhomologous (i.e., non-matching) chromosomes. During cell division, errors can occur in chromosome replication. A break that results in a rearrangement of chromosomal material where no material is lost is known as a *balanced translocation*. Other breaks can result in the loss of some chromosomal material. These are known as *unbalanced translocations*. Generally, there is a greater likelihood of morbidity with unbalanced translocations because there is either a gain or loss of some genetic material.

Within a single chromosome or matched chromosome pair, errors in chromosome replication can result in some genetic material being duplicated, deleted or flipped the wrong way (inverted). The extent of morbidity associated with these phenomena is highly variable. The ability of karyotyping to diagnose rearrangements, duplications, deletions or inversions depends on the size of the alteration. However, molecular techniques are now available that can identify smaller structural abnormalities with greater precision.

## Chromosomes Contain DNA

Chromosomes are made up of deoxyribonucleic acid (DNA) and protein. DNA is composed of complex chemical substances called *bases*. Combinations of the four bases (adenine (A), guanine (G), cytosine (C) and thymine (T)) arranged in a helical structure (like a spiral staircase) in a specific order define an individual's physical characteristics, susceptibility to disease and some behavioral characteristics. Chromosomes contain almost 3 billion base pairs of DNA that code for about 30,000-40,000 genes.

## DNA Codes for Protein

*Genes* are the sequences of DNA that code for proteins that comprise the structure and carry on the functions of all of the cells in the human body. The coding regions make up less than 5% of the genome. The function of the remaining DNA is not clear, but it is thought to have structural and regulatory function. That is, some of the sequence may code for binding sites for proteins which, when present in a particular form, can act to turn on or turn off (i.e., stimulate production or inhibition) another gene or protein in a biochemical cascade.

When signaled to produce a protein, the double-stranded DNA unwinds. An enzyme called RNA polymerase moves in between the strands, and uses one of the strands of DNA as a template for making a single stranded piece of RNA in a process called *transcription*. The RNA, called "messenger" RNA, carries the genetic information into the body of the cell, where it attaches to a ribosome. The ribosome brings together the building blocks for making the protein (amino acids) in a process called *translation*. Once attached to the ribosome, another type of RNA called *transfer* RNA brings individual amino acids to the ribosome. The amino acids are chemically bonded together to form the protein. When translation is complete, the protein falls off of the ribosome, and self-assembles into a three dimensional shape. Sometimes, the protein structure will undergo additional modifications, such as binding with other protein structures to make a complex molecule that will perform a function for the cell.

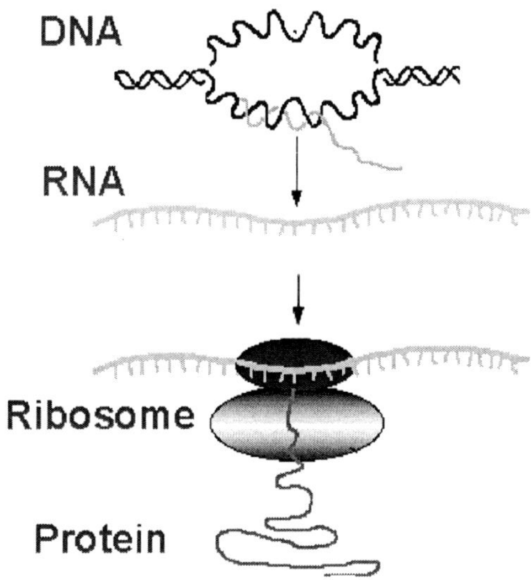


**Figure 2**. DNA Codes for Protein.
**Source**: Adapted from "The Central Dogma of Molecular Biology," Access Excellence @ the National Health Museum, © 1999, at [*http://www.access excellence.org/ AB/GG/ central.html*].

Because of the way that RNA is transcribed from DNA, then translated into a protein, the protein, although a different chemical composition than the DNA, reflects the sequence of the DNA. Thus, variations in the DNA sequence can manifest as variations in the protein. Some of the variations will alter the protein function. For example, a *mutation* may change the DNA code to tell the RNA polymerase to stop transcribing prematurely. The resulting protein would be too short, and would be unlikely to function. Normally, a "reading frame" consists of the DNA that is going be transcribed and translated. The polymerase enzyme reads three bases at a time to code for each amino acid. A mutation that deletes a base will throw off the reading frame. The resulting protein may be comprised of a nonsensical — or "mis-sense" — sequence that has no function. Other mutations may result in a base change that substitutes one amino acid for another. In this case, the function of the resulting protein could be almost normal (if the amino acids were very similar in structure) or could be impaired (if they were different). Some mutations may occur in regulatory sequences of DNA, which control how much and when a protein is produced.

## Genotype Influences Phenotype

Though most of the genome is very similar between individuals, there can be significant variation in physical appearance or function between individuals. Genes can have several different forms, called *alleles* which account for much of the variation. The specific alleles that are present on the chromosome pair constitutes the person's *genotype.* The actual observable physical trait is known as the *phenotype.* For example, having one brown-eye color allele and one blue eye color allele would be an example of a genotype and brown eyes would be the phenotype.[18]

Many complex factors affect how a genotype (DNA) translates to a phenotype (observable trait) in ways that are not yet clear for many traits or conditions. Study of a person's genotype may determine if a person has a mutation associated with a disease, but only observation of the phenotype can determine if that person actually has physical characteristics or symptoms of the disease. Generally, the risk of developing symptoms associated with a single mutation or trait can be more easily assessed because they are inherited in a predictable fashion (also known as Mendelian inheritance) compared to those associated with either multiple mutations in multiple genes, or traits or conditions that are acquired over time. Complex diseases, such as heart disease, cancer, immune disorders, or mental illness, for example, have both inherited and environmental components that are very difficult to separate. Thus, it can be difficult to determine whether an individual will develop symptoms, how severe the symptoms may be, or when they may appear.

## What Is a Genetic Test?

Scientifically, a genetic test is defined as "an analysis performed on human DNA, RNA, genes, and/or chromosomes to detect heritable or acquired genotypes, mutations, phenotypes, or karyotypes that cause or are likely to cause a specific disease or condition. A genetic test also is the analysis of human proteins and certain metabolites, which are predominantly used to detect heritable or acquired genotypes, mutations, or phenotypes."[19] Once the sequence of a gene is known, looking for the specific changes is relatively straightforward using a number of scientific methods. In fact, the methods have become so advanced that hundreds or thousands of genetic variations can be detected simultaneously.

Most clinical genetic tests are for rare disorders, but increasingly, tests are becoming available to determine susceptibility for future disease, or responses to different medications. Genetic tests can predict risks of disease, screen newborns for metabolic or inherited conditions, identify carriers, establish prenatal or clinical diagnoses or prognoses in individuals, families, or populations or direct clinical management. Tests that are used primarily for other purposes, but that may contribute to diagnosing a genetic disease (e.g., blood smear, certain serum chemistries), or tests for forensic purposes are not included in this definition.

Assessing how well a genetic test works requires determining the association between the genetic variation and the disease, condition or trait of interest. Some important measures of association are the clinical sensitivity, clinical specificity, and the positive predictive value.[20] The *clinical sensitivity* of a test describes how often a test is positive when the disease, condition or trait is present. The *clinical specificity* describes how often the test will be negative when the disease, condition or trait is absent. A *false negative* result occurs when the test is negative, but the disease is present. False negative results can occur because the test did not work properly, or because a different genetic marker — not the one detected by the test —caused the disease. A *false positive* result occurs when the test is positive, but the disease is not present. False positive results can occur because the test detected something nonspecific (not related to the condition at all) or because of incomplete penetrance,[21] variable expressivity,[22] or because the marker is predictive — that is, the disease has not occurred yet. The *positive predictive value* of a test is the proportion of times that an individual has a disease, given that the test was positive. The positive predictive value is a measure of confidence in how closely associated the test result is with the trait of interest — a high positive predictive value means that a person with a positive result is likely to have (or get) the disease.[23]

## Genetic Tests Can Have Variable Clinical Utility

Single gene disorders, such as sickle cell anemia or cystic fibrosis (CF), result from changes in one gene. A single genetic change in the hemoglobin gene results in sickle cell anemia. The associations are straightforward and the positive predictive value of the test, given that there are two copies of the mutation, is nearly 100%. In contrast, while CF is a single gene disorder, over 1,000 mutations in the CF gene have been associated with various forms of the disease. The American College of Medical Genetics (ACMG) has recommended a panel of 25 mutations, which can detect 80-95% of Caucasian people who have at least one copy of a gene that can cause CF. Using the test panel of 25 mutations, the test could be negative, but the individual could still have a mutation that is not detectable using the panel. The detection rate varies with ethnicity, so the test of 25 mutations has a different predictive value in individuals with different ethnic backgrounds.[24] As with many other genetic tests, a difference in test performance among ethnicities creates the potential for differential treatment of a person or group of persons based on their similar genetic information.

The positive predictive value of predictive genetic markers are particularly difficult to assess because of the long time it takes for the condition to develop. Mutations can arise spontaneously (called acquired mutations) or can be inherited. For some tests, like one for the BRCA gene that is associated with a predisposition to breast cancer, information has accumulated over the past 14 years to demonstrate the predictive value of the test results. While 2% of individuals in the general population develop breast or ovarian cancer by age 50, 33-50% of individuals with a family history of cancer and a BRCA mutation will develop breast or ovarian cancer by age 50.[25]

## GENETIC TESTS ARE AVAILABLE

As of March 14, 4, 2005, 578 laboratories were offering genetic tests for 1,109 diseases. Of those tests, 793 are available for clinical diagnosis, while 316 are available for research only.[26] Asked about realistic promise of genetic technology, Francis Collins, the Director of the National Institute for Human Genome Research predicts, "I think we can count on the availability within the next decade of a panel of genetic tests that are going to be offered to all of us to determine our risk of common illnesses, focused particularly on those diseases for which there is some intervention available for those found to be at high risk."[27]

## GENETIC TESTS ARE REGULATED BY THE FEDERAL GOVERNMENT

The Food and Drug Administration (FDA) regulates genetic tests that are manufactured by industry and sold for clinical diagnostic use.[28] These test kits usually come prepackaged with all of the reagents and instructions that a laboratory needs to perform the test. FDA requires manufacturers of the kits to make sure that the test detects what they say it will, in the patient population in which they intend the test to be used. Depending on the perceived risk associated with the intended use promoted by the manufacturer, genetic tests must either prove that they are safe and effective, or that they are substantially equivalent to something that is already on the market that has the same intended use. As of March 14, 2005, only 11 genetic test kits have been approved or cleared by the FDA.

Most genetic tests are performed, not with test kits, but rather as laboratory testing services (or "homebrew" tests), meaning that clinical laboratories themselves make the reagents used in the tests. Clinical laboratories must conform to the provisions of the Clinical Laboratory Improvement Act of 1988 (CLIA). CLIA is administered by the Center for Medicare and Medicaid Services (CMS) and the Centers for Disease Control and Prevention (CDC). FDA determines the category of complexity of the test so that laboratories know which parts of CLIA they must follow. CLIA generally establishes requirements for laboratory processes, such as personnel training and quality control/quality assurance programs. CLIA requires laboratories to prove that their tests work properly, to maintain the appropriate documentation, and to show that tests are interpreted by laboratory professionals with the appropriate training. However, unlike FDA, CLIA does not require that tests made by laboratories undergo any review by an outside agency to see if they work properly. Proponents of CLIA argue that regulation of the testing process (versus the actual test that FDA reviews) gives the laboratories optimal flexibility to modify tests as new information becomes available, without requiring that every change be reviewed by FDA. Critics argue that CLIA does not go far enough to assure the accuracy of genetic tests.

## SOME CLINICAL GENETIC TESTS ARE COVERED BY HEALTH INSURERS

Health insurers are playing an increasingly large role in determining which medical tests are available by deciding which tests they will pay for as part of patient benefit packages. They go one step further than FDA in assessing the utility of any new medical product or service. While insurers require that a test be approved by FDA (when required), they also want evidence that it is "medically necessary;" that is, evidence exists to demonstrate that the test will affect a patient's health outcome in a positive way.[29] This additional requirement of documented health outcomes underscores the importance of patient participation in long-term research in genetic medicine. Particularly for genetic tests, many of which can be conducted on most human tissue specimens from conception to death, data on health outcomes may take a very long time to collect.

*Chapter 3*

# HEALTH INFORMATION

Health information is currently used by health insurers and employers. The use of the information is regulated by several different laws. Understanding how health information is currently used and regulated provides a framework for discussion of whether extra protections are necessary for genetic information, and if so, which protections are most appropriate.

## USE OF HEALTH INFORMATION BY HEALTH INSURERS

Standard health insurance practice currently uses family history in the process of placing individuals (or groups) in a risk category for determining their premiums (underwriting). Individuals (or groups) at higher risk are charged higher premiums to cover the anticipated costs of their care. Traditional approaches to underwriting also use age, sex, type of occupation, financial stability of a group, employee turnover and prior cost (of care) experience to determine what a group's insurance premium should be. In general, premiums for a large group with one or two sick members can remain relatively stable, as the cost of the sick individuals is spread amongst all members of the group. However, as groups become smaller, the cost of insurance for the group is more dependent on the health of the individual group members, since one sick individual in a small group can result in high premiums for the whole group. Individuals who are not part of a group (outside of a family) must bear the entire premium increase associated with any illness, thus making insurance prohibitively expensive for many sick individuals.

Insurers state that most genetic information is not useful to the underwriting process, because the clinical significance and relationship to the severity of illness is not known for many conditions. However, some actuaries agree that adding diagnostic information significantly improves the power of traditional underwriting methods to predict future medical expense.[30] Furthermore, since insurance companies already use health information, they believe they should be able to use genetic information when the link to future illness (and the costs thereof) is predictable.

Lowden[31] provides examples of how genetic information (including family history) can be used to underwrite diseases like Huntington's, breast cancer and hereditary colon cancer for life insurance. Some health care providers and consumers fear that Lowden's model could also be applied to health (or medical expense) insurance. In the model, persons without a mutation are charged standard rates, while asymptomatic carriers of mutations, in the presence of family history, are charged higher premiums to cover the higher mortality which is associated with their condition. The lower the likelihood that the disease will manifest and cause premature death, the smaller the increase in premium. For example, the premium for a person with Huntington's Disease, which causes disease 100% of the time, would be higher than that of a person with a BRCA mutation, which is associated with premature death only 25% of the time. Lowden suggests that insurers support screening for mutations for which preventive interventions can reduce the risk of death. However, health insurers may disagree, depending on the nature, expense and effectiveness of the interventions in preventing symptoms and other medical costs of treating an acute or chronic illness; that which reduces the risk of death, may not reduce health or disability expenses (and lower life insurance premiums).

Insurers are concerned about adverse selection. Adverse selection occurs when individuals have information about their genetic risk and they purchase health, life or disability insurance at lower rates and without disclosing that information to the insurer. This practice threatens financial solvency of insurance companies because individuals are able to obtain insurance at low premiums that do not accurately reflect their risk of expenditures.[32]

## USE OF HEALTH INFORMATION BY EMPLOYERS

Employers are permitted to require medical examinations of prospective employees who have been given conditional offers of employment, if all employees in a similar situation are given the medical exam. They are also permitted to receive information related to applicants' or employees' current disability or health status when the information is related to the individuals' abilities to do their job.[33] However, the Americans with Disabilities Act (ADA) prohibits employers from revoking an offer, or from making other promotion decisions on the basis of that health information. Though genetics is not specifically addressed by the ADA, the Equal Employment Opportunities Commission (EEOC) interprets the ADA to mean that employees and/or job applicants cannot be required to undergo genetic screening. Supporters of the new legislation argue that because ADA does not explicitly address genetics, the protections that would be applied by the court system are not clear.[34] Opponents believe that the ADA is sufficient, and that the new legislation is not clear on workplace situations where an employee's genetic makeup could interfere with the major functions of the individual's job or put others at risk of harm.

*Chapter 4*

# WHAT IS GENETIC INFORMATION?

The definition of genetic information varies among sources. It is generally described as the information from a genetic test about genes, gene products, inherited characteristics or other traits that are derived from an individual or an individual's family member(s). Information about an individual's current health status (such as sex, age, results of physical examination, and chemical, blood, or urine analysis —where the analyses do not provide information about an individual's genotype) is generally not considered to be genetic information. It is important for lawmakers to understand the scope of different definitions, as the broader the definition the more expansive the prohibitions on discrimination.

## THE GENETIC TEST RESULT

By a narrow definition, genetic information is derived from a genetic test. Genetic tests, when performed on most normal body tissues or cells (i.e., blood or cheek swab, fetal or embryonic cells) provide information about the individual's genes that were inherited from their mother and father. Individuals cannot help or change their inherited genetic make-up (at least with today's scientific capabilities). In this manner, DNA-based testing of inherited genetic variants differs from other medical testing in important ways: it can have exceptionally long-range predictive powers over the lifespan of an individual; it can predict disease or increased risk for disease in the absence of clinical signs or symptoms; it can reveal the sharing of genetic variants within families at precise and calculable rates; and, at least theoretically, it has the potential to generate a unique identifier profile for individuals. Also unlike most other medical tests, the stability of DNA means that most genetic tests can be performed on material from a body (such as the root of a human hair) and continue to provide information after the individual has died.

Genetic tests can also be performed on the DNA, RNA or protein of tissue that has been altered by disease (such as a tumor) and provide information about the disease process. Sometimes, the disease process results in genetic changes, or conversely, genetic changes (such as a result of an exposure to a toxic or infectious agent) can result in disease. These genetic changes are said to be *acquired* because they occur only in the disease tissue, and not in the rest of the body's cells.

Tests that are performed for acquired genetic markers that occur with a disease have implications only for individuals with the disease, and not family members. In general, tests to determine what genes are turned on and off, and what gene products are made in diseased tissue in response to medication are called "pharmacogenomic" tests. For example, a tumor may have acquired genetic changes that make it different from normal host tissue that may also render that tumor susceptible or resistant to chemotherapy. Some argue that genetic tests to determine if an individual is likely to have an adverse effect of a medication (also known as pharmacogenetic tests) are different from genetic tests for heritable disease or susceptibility to disease. While pharmacogenetic information may not have the same stigma associated with it that tests to determine whether or not someone has (or will get) a disease, the results could provide unintentional information about other unrelated characteristics that could also apply to family members.

Tests on gene products, notably RNA and protein, usually provide more limited information about the current state of biochemical health much like other laboratory analyses. However, in some situations, they can indirectly provide information about what is happening at the DNA level. For example, a particular protein may be missing or not functioning well because there is a mutation in the gene that codes for the protein. Alternatively, the protein problem could be caused by interference from some other factor related to disease or environment. High cholesterol may result because of abnormal genes that affect the body's ability to metabolize or make cholesterol, or it may simply be a result of too many saturated fats in an individual's diet.

## Family History

Defined more broadly, "family history is the first genetic test."[35] Family history of traits, diseases, or conditions, is also considered 'genetic' information by the medical community: if an individual has multiple relatives with a trait or disorder he/she may also have a higher than average risk of also having the trait or disorder. Particularly for complex traits or disorders, tests have not been developed or are not widely available for the exact genetic marker that causes or is associated with the disease. Instead of a direct test, health professionals can use other markers that 'run in the family' as a surrogate measure when they also run with the disease.

## Is Genetic Information Different from Other Medical Information?

Medical information is often presumed confidential, but increasing capabilities to store and rapidly transfer data escalate the challenge of protecting privacy. At issue is whether genetic information should be protected generally as a subset of medical or health data, or by special genetic privacy laws. Those making the case against special protections assert that genetic information is fundamentally no different than other health data and is already adequately protected by medical privacy laws. Proponents argue that genetic information warrants special protection because of its stability, unique predictive qualities, and the impact that public fear of discrimination is having on the behavior of patients and healthcare providers.

One study compared the experiences, attitudes and beliefs of persons with genetic conditions (cystic fibrosis and sickle cell disease) to those with other serious medical conditions (diabetes, HIV, breast cancer and colon cancer) and to persons at risk for developing a disease (breast or colon cancer) due to strong family history. The authors found that in most instances, patients felt strongly that their medical information needed to be protected regardless of whether the information was genetic or non-genetic medical information. In fact, respondents indicated that information about non-genetic stigmatizing conditions — such as abortion history, mental health history, drug and alcohol history, HIV status, and sexually transmitted disease —needed special protection. Based on their findings, the authors concluded that separate privacy policies for genetic and non-genetic medical information could be unwarranted.[36]

The Senate report for S. 1053 (S.Rept. 108-122), the genetic nondiscrimination bill that was passed by the Senate in 2003, acknowledged that eventually "it may not be possible or even desirable in health care delivery or scientific research to isolate genetic information as it pervades health information." Understanding the ways in which genetic information is like and unlike other types of information can help to inform the debate over the need for genetic-specific nondiscrimination legislation.

## IMPLICATIONS OF GENETIC INFORMATION FOR INDIVIDUALS

Like other medical information, genetic test results can be used to diagnosis a disease or condition. However, unlike most other medical tests, they can also be used to predict that a currently healthy person may develop a debilitating condition at some point later in their life. Alternatively, the information may only suggest that the individual may be susceptible to — or at risk for developing — a particular illness or condition. Some of these future conditions may not have an intervention that can alleviate, mitigate or prevent the condition from occurring. Many rely on individuals taking personal responsibility for their health related behaviors (i.e., avoiding fatty foods if they have a defined genetic risk for obesity or heart disease). Similar to other medical tests, inaccurate results can result in increasing a patient's anxiety level if they are positive, or give them a false sense of reassurance if the results are negative. A false genetic test result could cause a provider to make a wrong treatment decision. The provider could give a medicine to a patient that will not likely work for them or worse, cause them to experience an adverse event. Or, the provider could fail to give a medicine to a patient that could have alleviated their symptoms or disease.

Genetic testing may reveal unintentional information about a person, or information with unknown significance given current scientific limitations. In general, though health information may also be revealed through routine non-genetic medical testing (such as AIDS or pregnancy testing), the development of multiplex testing and gene chip technology, and of research linking genes with health characteristics, is enabling an increasingly cost effective mechanism for testing hundreds or even thousands of genetic health indicators at one time. Genetic testing on this scale could likely lead to the revelation of an enormous amount of unexpected health information about individuals, making true informed consent for each individual test prohibitively time consuming. Banking and storage of this vast amount of information, along with personal identifiers, provides unique challenges to privacy protections. Consumer advocates caution that although economic incentives favor testing for a large number of genetic characteristics at one time, testing should be limited to allow for thorough informed consent and genetic counseling.

Genetic information can be used not only for health care, but also to identify individuals with a high degree of certainty. Genetic information has been used to help convict and exonerate individuals accused of committing crimes. It has been used to help identify the remains of war and accident victims. Because of these potential applications, tissue samples and certain types of genetic information collected for health care purposes could be used in law enforcement, and vice versa. Knowledge that genetic information collected for health care may have forensic applications may help to guide lawmakers concerned with the availability and use of genetic information.

## Implications of Genetic Information for the Family

Like other medical tests, genetic tests for acquired markers have direct medical implications only for the individuals taking the tests. However, unlike other medical tests, genetic tests for inherited traits have implications for biological relatives of the individual. Parents, siblings and children have a predictable risk of sharing certain genetic markers. Furthermore, the unchanging nature of DNA means that genetic testing for inherited conditions can be performed at any stage of human development on most tissue types, offering the possibility of preimplantation or prenatal diagnosis, or fetal intervention.

It is more difficult determining risk to family members of a complex disorder (such as susceptibility to cancer, mental illness, or heart disease), because scientists have not yet been able to tease apart the relative influence of genetic and environmental factors in disease progression. Some genetic tests cannot be interpreted for an individual unless some members of their family are also tested.[37] In those cases, family members may or may not want to know their test results. Sometimes testing family members can provide evidence that an individual's paternity is not what he or she previously thought.

## IMPLICATIONS OF GENETIC INFORMATION FOR SOCIETY

Genetic information challenges traditional medical perceptions of health and disease, what is normal or abnormal, and raises questions about what constitutes "current" or "manifested" disease. These concepts are becoming increasingly blurred as scientists gain the ability to interpret genetic information with more resolution. For example, consider the trait of, intelligence or a biochemical process such as glucose metabolism. Human beings vary along a continuum of each, but at some point the extremes become pathologic. Many genetic conditions lead to mental retardation, and yet there are other genetic factors that influence low average to above average intelligence. Genetic factors have been associated with the development of diabetes.

Genetics may soon provide the opportunity to test large groups of people for disease susceptibilities and begin to devise health interventions to alleviate or mitigate the risk of or prevent or cure diseases. However, fear caused by the possibility that a job may be lost or insurance may be cancelled — whether real or perceived — is the primary reason individuals refrain from seeking what could be a beneficial genetic test in clinical or research settings.[38] As a result, the ability of scientists to gather the data that are necessary to determine the utility or ultimately the value in genetic testing for medicine is compromised. Furthermore, because the prevalence of disease causing genes often varies by ethnicity, there is potential for discrimination against groups of people that share similar genetic information.

Genetic information may be used in order to link a person to a distinct group or heritage. This type of information may have consequences, particularly for individuals who have rights based upon heritage, such as Native American Indians. Advocates of these groups are wary of the potential effect that genetic testing and information could have both on their current rights and protections, and on future discrimination against them. Others argue that definitions of race and heredity are irrelevant or that genetic testing will not supplant current non-genetic determinants of heredity.

Another societal issue has to do with scientific progress and implications both for privacy and for equity. In the privacy arena, a person could grant others access to genetic data that is benign by standards of today. However, with scientific advancements these same data may reveal more sensitive information. In the equity arena, those with health conditions for which genetic tests currently exist may suffer discrimination in the near future while those with similarly debilitating health conditions for which there is no genetic test may escape the same discrimination simply by virtue of the current state of science. While large-scale banking of some genetic information could have widespread public health benefit — such as facilitating characterization of genetic markers associated with rare adverse drug events — both of these potentialities should be of interest to those seeking to limit or facilitate access to genetic information.

*Chapter 5*

# What Evidence Is There That Genetic Discrimination Exists?

There have been few actual cases of genetic discrimination in health insurance and employment. Rothenbery and Terry[39] hypothesize that this is because: (1) the use of genetic information by employers and insurers is not widespread; (2) affected persons may not know the underlying basis for adverse employment or insurance decisions; and (3) many cases may go unreported because of disincentives associated with publicizing discrimination lawsuits.

## Cases of Genetic Discrimination

There have been a few studies on the prevalence of genetic discrimination in health insurance, employment, and other settings. One study reported that 22% of the respondents indicated that they or a family member were refused health insurance as a result of a genetic condition.[40] This study was strongly criticized by the Health Insurance Association of America (HIAA), which has argued that there is no evidence showing that insurers engage in genetic discrimination, and that federal legislation to prohibit discrimination based on genetic information is unnecessary.[41] However, another study found that a number of institutions, including health and life insurance companies, health care providers, blood banks, adoption agencies, the military and schools, were reported to have engaged in genetic discrimination against asymptomatic individuals. The alleged discriminatory practices included an insurance company treating a genetic diagnosis as a preexisting condition, an adoption agency refusing to allow a woman at risk for Huntington's disease to adopt a child, and an employer terminating an employee after the employee disclosed a risk of Huntington's disease.[42]

On October 18, 2004, several individuals shared stories of genetic discrimination with the Secretary's Advisory Committee on Genetics, Health and Society (SACGHS).[43] These cases are highlighted below.

- Phil Hardt has hemophilia B, a bleeding disorder, and Huntington's Disease. He testified that a human resource manager for an early employer had indicated that he should withhold information about his hemophilia and any bleeding episodes from his employer or he would never be promoted or trained. In addition, he indicated that his daughter was unable to receive mortgage life insurance unless she tested negative for Huntington's Disease. His grandson was denied health insurance because of the hemophilia B that he inherited, and that his was forced to accept lower wages so that they could qualify for state welfare and insurance coverage. Two of his other children decided to pay out of pocket, and to be tested anonymously for Huntington's Disease to protect them from discrimination. Mr. Hardt since applied — and was rejected — for long-term care insurance.
- Rebecca Fisher, a mother and early-breast cancer survivor with a strong family history recounted how her employer, a small, self-insured community hospital, was more concerned that the cost of her bone marrow transplantation and other health care had exceeded the cap for that year than with her health or productivity.
- Tonia Phillips, a woman with a BRCA-1 mutation in her family, chose to undergo prophylactic surgery to reduce her risk of breast and/or ovarian cancer. After her procedures, her employer's health insurance policy had increased by $13,000 for four people. Her employer asked her to switch to her husband's policy, and in doing so, indicated that she would receive a wage increase.
- Paula Funk, another individual who carried a BRCA-1 mutation, indicated that she and her family paid out of pocket for testing, and that her physicians and health care providers would not write her BRCA-1 status on insurance claims forms because of the potential for discrimination. She further testified regarding her difficulty in finding an insurance company that would cover herself and her husband, co-owners of a small business, as a group so that their

premiums would be affordable, given her family history and genetic testing status.

- Heidi Williams, an individual diagnosed with alpha-1 antitrypsin deficiency,[44] also spoke at a press conference at the House of Representatives on April 1, 2004; she explained that a large health insurance company (Humana) had denied health insurance coverage for her two children on the basis that they were carriers of alpha-1 antitrypsin disease. Carriers only have one copy of an abnormal gene, and do not exhibit symptoms of the disease. After receiving inquiries from the Genetic Alliance (a consumer advocacy organization) and the press, the insurance company reversed its decision to deny coverage, and provided six months of free coverage.

On July 20, 2000, Terri Seargent, also an individual diagnosed with alpha-1 antitrypsin deficiency, filed a statement with the Senate Health, Education, Labor and Pension Committee indicating that soon after her diagnosis, she was unexpectantly released from employment. Without a job, and having a pre-existing condition, she also lost her health, life and disability insurance. Later, an investigation by the Equal Employment Opportunity Commission (EEOC) supported her allegation of discrimination under the Americans with Disabilities Act (ADA).[45]

## Genetic Testing by Employers

Though not yet believed to be a widespread practice, surveys of employer practice and employee experience indicate that there are some employers that test employees for genetic markers. No genetic employment discrimination cases have been decided in a federal court or the Supreme Court. However, several have been brought or threatened, and two cases were settled out of court.[46]

The American Management Association (AMA) has conducted several surveys of employer practices in medical testing in the workplace. In their 2001 survey, the AMA found that 68% of major U.S. firms require medical examinations for new hires, current employees, or both. These are most frequently required in public administration and manufacturing positions and less frequently in business or professional positions. Establishing "fitness for duty" is the leading reason that firms engage in complete medical examinations (48% of respondents). According to a revised version of their annual survey, 1.3% of companies test new or current employees for sickle cell anemia, 0.4% test for Huntington's Disease, and 20.1% ask about family medical history. When asked if results (e.g., from employer test programs, or from testing done elsewhere) were used in hiring, reassigning, retaining or dismissing employees, 1.0% of employers indicated that the sickle cell, 0.8% indicated that Huntington's and 5.5% indicated that family history results were used in any regard.

In their 1998 survey, the AMA questioned the respondents' understanding of what constituted a genetic test. When presented with NIH's definition of genetic test — "an analysis of human DNA, RNA, chromosomes, proteins, and certain metabolites in order to detect heritable disease related genotypes, mutations, phenotypes, or karyotypes for clinical purposes. Such purposes include predicting risk of disease, identifying carriers, and establishing prenatal and clinical diagnosis or prognosis" — only two respondents (out of 1,627) indicated that they performed genetic testing. A larger percentage (14.3%) indicated testing for "susceptibility to workplace hazards." Upon further investigation, the AMA found that not all of the testing was "genetic testing." Followup interviews indicated that only nine of 44 employers who indicated having testing programs, actually had genetic testing programs. Apparently some employers thought that any blood test constituted "genetic testing;" others thought that diagnostic testing rather than susceptibility testing was "genetic testing."[47]

Employers have long been interested in identifying "optimal" employees using non-health characteristics — such as behavior (i.e., substance abuse, mental instability, compulsive disorders) or intelligence — to identify special skills or deficits that are predictive of productivity.[48] Though behavioral genetics is not ready for prime time testing (largely due to the very complex interaction of genes and the environment), other forms of testing are common. For example, the 2001 AMA survey found that testing for illegal substance use is the most common form of workplace testing, practiced by 67% of employers.

A study of 332 consumers who were members of genetic support groups found that 13% of respondents reported that they or another family member were denied a job or let go because of a genetic condition in the family.[49] The experience was significantly different for respondents who had a genetic condition (21%) compared to respondents who did not have a genetic condition (4%). Two examples were highlighted: one respondent, a man with a sex chromosome disorder, indicated that he was denied a job when a doctor wrote the name of the disorder on his medical report during his pre-employment physical. The potential employer told the applicant of the decision and, knowing it was illegal, also stated that they would deny the conversation. In the second example, a woman with a skeletal disorder reported that her employment was terminated after she informed her employer of her diagnosis. The woman sought legal counsel, and the termination was withdrawn.

In 2002, Burlington Northern Santa Fe Corporation, one of the country's biggest railroads, agreed to pay $2.2 million to settle charges that it had tested employees without their knowledge for a genetic marker dubiously associated with carpel tunnel syndrome (CTS). CTS is a painful hand and wrist condition often caused by repetitive motion. The company denied violating the law, and insisted that testing was necessary to determine the cause of injury to 36 employees who claimed to have job-related CTS (20 actually underwent testing before the program was voluntary suspended).[50] In 1998, Lawrence Berkeley Laboratory was accused of testing employees for syphilis, pregnancy and the sickle cell trait without their knowledge or consent. The case was settled in 1999.[51]

## OSHA

The Occupational Safety and Hazard Act (OSHA) establishes a legal duty for employers to protect employees from hazards in the workplace. Although the statute does not require an employer to perform particular tests, the employer may choose to implement programs that monitor employees' potential exposure to toxic or hazardous elements. Standards for these programs, found in 29 C.F.R. Part 1910, allow for genetic testing:

> Such a program could include genetic testing to evaluate employees for acquired genetic changes resulting from an exposure in order to control adverse outcomes and minimize exposure to hypersensitive persons.

Genetic monitoring for acquired damage resulting from exposure to a toxic element is different from genetic screening for an inherited predisposition to an occupationally related disease.[52] For example, monitoring may be used to determine if an employee is developing damage from being exposed to asbestos. On the other hand, a different type of test could potentially determine if the employee was more susceptible to asbestos damage to begin with. The distinction may be relevant in future disagreements concerning whether any ill-health effects sustained by the worker were a result of the job exposure, or if they were caused by something the worker "was born with."

For work areas using regulated, known carcinogens (i.e., cancer-causing agents), OSHA requires that:

> before an employee is assigned to enter a regulated area, a preassignment physical examination by a physician shall be provided. The examination shall include the personal history of the employee, family and occupational background, including genetic and environmental factors. ... Employers of employees examined pursuant to this paragraph shall cause to be maintained complete and accurate records of all such medical examinations. Records shall be maintained for the duration of the employee's employment.[53]

The following excerpts are from two examples of OSHA recommendations regarding exposure to specific toxic elements.

For lead:

> the medical history is also of fundamental importance and should include a listing of all past and current medical conditions, current medications including proprietary drug intake, previous surgeries and hospitalizations, allergies, smoking history, alcohol consumption, and also non-occupational lead exposures such as hobbies (hunting, riflery). Also known childhood exposures should be elicited. Any previous history of hematological, neurological, gastrointestinal, renal, psychological, gynecological, genetic, or reproductive problems should be specifically noted.

For ethylene oxide (EtO):

> clinical evidence of adverse effects associated with the exposure to EtO is present in the form of increased incidence of cancer in laboratory animals (leukemia, stomach, brain), mutation in offspring in animals, and resorptions and spontaneous abortions in animals and human populations respectively. Findings in humans and experimental animals exposed to airborne concentrations of EtO also indicate damage to the genetic material (DNA). These include hemoglobin alkylation, unsecheduled DNA synthesis, sister chromatid exchange chromosomal aberration, and functional sperm abnormalities.

## IMPACT OF THE FEAR OF DISCRIMINATION ON BEHAVIOR

While there are few documented cases of discrimination, studies have shown that public fear of discrimination influences the uptake of genetic testing and the use of genetic information by consumers and health professionals. On January 27, 2000, the Secretary's Advisory Committee on Genetic Testing (SACGT) sponsored a public forum to gather perspectives on issues in genetic testing. Many comments were received from patients, consumers, health professionals, scientists, genetic test developers, educators, industry representatives, policymakers, lawyers, students and others representing a wide range of diverse ethnic and racial groups.[54] Comments were also received from a mailing to 2500 individuals and organizations and a website consultation requesting feedback on several issues. The comments revealed several anecdotal cases of discrimination, and resulted in the committee forwarding two letters to the Secretary of Health and Human Services (HHS) urging support for nondiscrimination protections:

> During consultations with the public SACGT heard from many Americans who are concerned about the misuse of genetic information by third parties, such as health insurers and employers, and the potential for discrimination based on that information. Many stated that fear of genetic discrimination would dissuade them from undergoing a genetic test or participating in genetic research studies. Others stated that they would pay out of pocket for a genetic test to prevent the results from being placed in their medical record. Such concerns are a deterrent to advances in the field of genetic testing and may limit the realization of the benefits of genetic testing.[55]

At the October 18, 2004 meeting of SACGHS, several individuals testified about how their fears of discrimination affected their behavior:[56]

- Carolina Hinestrosa, a 10-year, two-time survivor of breast cancer and executive vice president for programs and planning of the National Breast Cancer Coalition stated that despite her strong personal and family history, she has not undergone genetic testing for fear of discrimination against herself and her daughter.

- A mother, Phaedra Malatek, described how her family has not taken advantage of the health benefits of genetic testing for hemochromatosis that ran in her family because of their fear of losing their health insurance, and possible discrimination against her children when they seek employment.

Surveys of professionals and patients suggest that individuals are most likely to withhold information about genetic testing from insurance companies and their employers. A survey of genetic counselors[57] found that, should counselors themselves be at risk of developing either breast cancer or hereditary non-polyposis colon cancer, most (108/159) would not submit charges to their insurance companies primarily because of the fear of discrimination. Twenty-five percent would use an alias when obtaining a test to reduce the risk of discrimination and maximize confidentiality. Most respondents indicated that, while they would share results with their physicians, family, and friends; sixty percent would not share the information with colleagues because of the need for privacy and fear of job discrimination based on the result.[58]

Of 91 participants in a study on hereditary pancreatitis, 22% believed that knowing their test results "might lead to medical insurance discrimination" for themselves or their families. While most individuals would share information with a physician or their family, only 4% indicated they would share results with their insurance companies, and 20% would shared them with their employers.[59] Another study of 98 extended families with history of breast or ovarian cancer, reported on 716 of 1,315 individuals who underwent counseling and DNA testing. Before receiving results, about half were concerned about insurance discrimination, and 1% indicated that they felt strongly that their family history of cancer had been the basis for insurance discrimination.[60]

A group of scientists at the University of Michigan offered gene testing for susceptibility to breast cancer to 184 individuals participating in a cancer risk evaluation clinic. Patients were charged about $225 for the initial consultation, and were required to pay Myriad Genetics directly for any testing they pursued. At the time, Myriad charged $395 for analysis of a single mutation, $450 for analysis of three common mutations found in individuals of Ashekenazi Jewish descent, and $2,400 for full sequencing of the breast cancer susceptibility genes (also called BRCA1 and 2). Patients had the option of self-paying, or billing their insurance companies. Though discussion of potential discrimination was standard practice in the counseling session that accompanied testing, the researchers only counted concerns initiated by the patient during the session. Of the 184 patients, 106 underwent testing. Of the 78 patients who declined testing, 48 (or 26% of the original cohort of 184) declined due to concerns about cost, confidentiality or insurance discrimination.[61] The authors found it difficult to separate concerns about cost, confidentiality and fear of insurance discrimination. Although a patient may have wanted to self-pay for fear of potential discrimination, the high cost of testing may have forced the patient to choose to bill insurance, or decline testing. The authors estimated that approximately 14% of patients eligible for testing would have had a BRCA mutation, but would not undergo testing because of cost, discrimination, or confidentiality concerns.

A follow-up telephone interview was conducted with 92 of the 184 patients concerning their actual experiences with their insurance companies. Of the 92, 15% paid out of pocket, intentionally not involving their insurance companies, while 38% (35 of 92) indicated that they did not have any problems obtaining coverage for the services requested. However, of those 35 patients, 23 only requested payment for the consult and surgery — not the testing — from their insurers. The remaining 47% experienced various difficulties in obtaining coverage for some or all of the services. The patient's family income was a significant factor in the decision to seek insurance reimbursement. In another study of 68 patients offered genetic testing for breast cancer, while 18 had access to free testing, and 13 sought insurance reimbursement, the remaining 37 chose to pay out of pocket citing concerns over insurability and confidentiality reasons.[62]

Concerns about discrimination may be lower amongst those with the lowest income who were covered by government programs, such as Medicaid, because eligibility does not depend on health status or underwriting decisions.[63]

When viewing evidence of the ways in which fear of genetic discrimination affects behavior, some have questioned whether genetic counseling itself may inadvertently add to the fear. The risk of discrimination by employers and insurers is often discussed in the counseling session that accompanies testing. Most counselors typically spend up to 15 minutes of a one- to two-hour counseling session discussing patient concerns about discrimination, even in states with more comprehensive anti-discrimination laws. Counselors typically note that actual cases of discrimination are few, and will provide information regarding the various legal protections.[64] While many counselors indicate that a significant proportion (25-50%) of patients may decline testing due to potential discrimination, other patients accept testing because the benefits of the information to their health or the health of a relative outweigh the risk of discrimination. Either way, counselors note that the potential risk adds to an already stressful situation.

In order to reassure patients about privacy, genetic counselors may vary their practices in several ways: they may be discreet about how a visit is documented (i.e., for cancer screening, not genetic testing); they may not send the results to the referring physician unless asked specifically by the patient to do so; or, they may request that the physician keep the results in a separate medical record. Some will forward coded samples to the laboratories for testing. Many genetic counselors will themselves maintain patient files that are separate from the rest of the hospital or medical center's records to minimize the possibility that an insurer will obtain genetic information in the process of reviewing a medical record for reimbursement.[65]

Genetic counselors note that the fears associated with predictive testing for future adult onset illness are not as apparent in testing in the prenatal and pediatric populations. Presumably this is because of the "crisis atmosphere" created with the diagnosis of a potential birth defect and the parents' decision of whether or not to terminate a pregnancy. In some cases including those involving newborns, the fear of insurability may be mitigated by the fact that children are covered under their parents' policies. However, some counselors have expressed concern about the way in which genetic information will be viewed when children become adults and have to find insurance on their own.[66]

*Chapter 6*

# How Do S. 306 and H.R. 1227 Compare to Existing Law?

Currently a number of federal laws touch the issues raised by the use of genetic information:[67] the ADA, Title VII of the Civil Rights Act of 1963, the Health Insurance Portability and Accountability Act (HIPAA) and Executive Order 13145. The ADA protects people from discrimination based on existing disability, history of disability, and perception of disability in employment. The executive order extends ADA prohibitions (including those based on genetic information) to federal agencies acting as employers. The HIPAA privacy regulations restrict the disclosure of health information, including genetic information, by group health plans. HIPAA also allows group health plans to use some health information (which could presumably include genetic information) in underwriting. HIPAA also limits denial of coverage based on pre-existing conditions to 12 months. In the absence of a current diagnosis, HIPAA would not include genetic information as a pre-existing condition. The Civil Rights Act provides some protections against genetic discrimination against members of a protected group, such as persons of a certain race, color, religion, sex or national origin.[68]

The existence and scope of state anti-discrimination legislation that could be interpreted to explicitly or implicitly cover genetics varies.[69] Most laws prohibit: (i) discrimination based on particular traits or diseases; or (ii) discrimination based on genetic test results; or (iii) insurers or employers from requiring that an individual take a genetic test and using the results.[70]

The proposed legislation before the 109th Congress, S. 306 and H.R. 1227, would extend current federal protections against discrimination to health insurers in the individual market, and would further limit the use and disclosure of genetic information. The bills would also bar insurers from using genetic information or family history of disease in underwriting for an individual (as an individual or applied to a group); however, insurers could still use genetic information as it is excepted from the definition of genetic test for every person enrolled in a group consistent with current law.[71]

Opponents of enacting special legislation to prevent potential discrimination on the basis of genetic information argue that current federal and state protections are sufficient. However, the current bills that the existing patchwork of state and federal laws is confusing, and inadequate to protect individuals from discrimination. Many professional and consumer groups believe that individuals should not be penalized in their ability to obtain insurance or a job because medical science can identify a trait, but cannot yet do much to treat it; for example, the American Civil Liberties Union (ACLU) stated at a hearing in 2001 that "Americans should be judged on their actual abilities, not their potential disabilities."[72] Supporters argue that without proper protections, individuals will continue to be afraid to participate in the very research that would allow scientists to discover treatments or lifestyle modifications to mitigate the negative or harmful effects of specific genes. Others argue that because existing federal laws have not been tested in court, the extent of their protection of genetic information is not clear. None of the existing laws or proposed bills address life or disability insurance.

*Chapter 7*

# HOW WOULD THE PROPOSED LEGISLATION PROTECT "GENETIC INFORMATION"?

In S. 306 and H.R. 1227 (which are identical), the protections for genetic information are primarily restrictions on the type of and manner in which genetic information could been used in determining eligibility for health insurance, establishing premiums for health insurance, and in making decisions regarding employment. The protections would apply to information derived from a genetic test done on individuals or their family members, and to information related to the occurrence of a disease or disorder in family members of the individual. The bills would clarify that genetic information would include the fact that an individual (or his/her family member) had taken a genetic test. The definition of genetic test in the bills is more restrictive than the medical or scientific definition of genetic test, which covers both predictive and diagnostic reasons for testing.[73] The bills focus on protecting predictive information (i.e., information about a future or potential health state in a currently symptom-free individual). Use of genetic information that is indicative of "manifested disease" is generally permitted in accordance with current law governing insurance and employment practices. This type of genetic information could be obtained from a diagnostic test.

Genetic information goes beyond what a test can determine to include family history and traits that 'run in a family' but for which a specific test has not been developed, is not widely available, or is not related to a disease. The bills stress the importance of family history. S.Rept. 108-122 for S. 1053 in the 108th Congress stated that "the committee realizes that family medical history could be used as a surrogate for a genetic trait by a health plan or health insurance issuer ... it is important to include family medical history in the definition of genetic information." The report further clarified the concept of family medical history as being consistent with the American Medical Association definition, and expected that the definition would evolve over time.

The bills restrict protections by limiting the definition of genetic test (see **Table 1**). They specifically exclude from Title I (health insurance provisions) medical information that is not genetic information, including the analysis of *protein or metabolites directly related to manifested disease*, disorder, or pathological condition. This exemption is not present in Title II (employment provisions). The protections apply to predictive, heritable genetic tests that provide information regarding a future or possible health status of a currently non-affected person. Both bills prohibit discrimination based on an individual's predictive test result (e.g., BRCA or breast cancer susceptibility), or the fact that a person's parent had Huntington's disease as long as that individual did not manifest the condition. Once a person becomes symptomatic, information derived from a person's DNA or RNA tests would still be protected under the proposed legislation; however, information derived from a protein or metabolite would be excepted. Health insurers would still be permitted to use or disclose the individual's current health status (as determined without a genetic test), consistent with existing law. The exception is not present in Title II, as employers are prohibited from using a person's current health status in specific ways by existing law.

**Table 1. The Definition of Genetic Test and Genetic Information in Title I and Title II of S. 306 and H.R. 1227**

| | **Title I** | **Title II** |
|---|---|---|
| | **Health Insurance** | **Employment** |
| **Genetic test** | The term "genetic test" means the analysis of human DNA, RNA, chromosomes, proteins or metabolites that detects genotypes, mutations, or chromosomal changes. | Same as Title I. |
| **Limitations or exemptions** | "Genetic test" does not mean:<br>(i) an analysis of proteins or metabolites that does not detect genotypes, mutations, or chromosomal changes; or<br>(ii) an analysis of proteins or metabolites that is directly related to a manifested disease, disorder, or pathological condition that could reasonably be detected by a health care professional with appropriate training and expertise in the field of medicine involved. | 'Genetic test' does not mean an analysis of proteins or metabolites that does not detect genotypes, mutations, or chromosomal changes. |
| **Genetic information** | "Genetic information" means:<br>(i) information about an individual's genetic tests;<br>(ii) information about genetic tests of family members of the individual;<br>(ii) information about the occurrence of a disease or disorder in family members | Same as Title I. |
| **Limitations or exemptions** | "Genetic information" does not include information about the age or sex of an individual. | Same as Title I. |

**Table 2. Examples of Genetic Testing Scenarios and Protected Information Under S. 306 and H.R. 1227**

| Scenario | S. 306 and H.R. 1227 |
| --- | --- |
| Test of tumor proteins; information is diagnostic, the tumor has not been removed. | **Not Protected** because "analysis is of protein is directly related to a manifestted disease." |
| Test of tumor DNA; information is diagnostic, the tumor has not been removed. | **Protected,** meets basic criteria for genetic test (only protein or metabolite tests meet exclusion for manifested disease). |
| Test of tumor proteins; tumor has been removed, information indicates the likelihood of tumor recurrence | **Not Protected** if the removed tumor is a "manifested disease." **Protected** if tumor removal means that the disease is no longer Manifested. |
| Test of tumor DNA; tumor has been removed; information indicates the likelihood of tumor recurrence. | **Protected**, meets basic criteria for genetic test, so"manifested" is not an issue; applies to tests of protein. |
| Test of tumor protein; information is response/resistance to therapy | **Not Protected** if information about possible drug response is considered "directly related to manifested disease."<br>**Protected** if not directly related. |
| Test of tumor on patient's DNA; Information is response/resistance to therapy. | **Protected**, meets basic criteria for genetic test, so "directly related" is not an issue (only protein or metabolite tests meet exclusion for manifested disease. |

One unique aspect of a genetic test result is that the same information can be both diagnostic and predictive depending on the situation. Consider a person with cancer. A genetic test of the tumor material provides information about the tumor, and its likelihood of recurrence. Surgery is performed to remove the tumor. The patient is in remission. Applying the definition in the bills, the following interpretations would be possible. The scenarios describe both diagnostic, predictive and pharmacogenomic applications for protein and DNA tests.

The definition of what constitutes a manifested disease has important bearing on the scope of protections of genetic information, particularly after a disease is "cured" or is in remission. From the example above, if a tumor has not been removed, test results on tumor *proteins* that could predict the likelihood that a tumor would recur may not be protected under the bills because analyses of *proteins* directly related to a *manifested disease* (the tumor) are excluded from the definition of genetic tests. However, if the same information is gained based on a DNA test, it would be protected information. Protections are unclear, for example, for information suggesting a likelihood of recurrence of a tumor that has been surgically removed. Once removed, would the tumor still be considered to be a manifested disease? Would genetic information gained from testing the tumor be protected if it indicated that the development of future tumors or other diseases is likely? By contrast, if a person underwent a genetic test to determine whether they were susceptible to adverse reactions from a certain treatment, would their test results be protected? Would it matter if they had a disease for which the treatment was indicated? Recall from a previous section, "The Genetic Test Result," that pharmacogenetic tests for individual susceptibilities to certain drugs can be performed at any point in an individual's life. Information from these tests reveals normal variability in how different people's bodies process different medications. The information is useful when obtained before a particular therapy is considered (i.e., when an individual does not have a manifested disease). Under the current definition it is possible that, in the presence of manifested disease, information that a person would *not* likely respond to a drug could potentially be used in a negative manner by health insurers. This concern is especially great if only one treatment exists.

## SCOPE OF COVERAGE: DEFINITION OF "FAMILY MEMBERS"

The risk of sharing genetic traits or conditions is greatest to first and second-degree blood relatives.[74] The risk of sharing genes decreases as the blood relationship becomes more distant. For example, first degree relatives share one-half of their genetic material, second degree relatives share one-fourth, and third degree relatives (first cousins), share one-eighth. Fourth cousins, which are ninth degree relatives, share only 1/512 of their genetic material. At this level of relationship, only very rare conditions appear more frequently in family members, and the risk of many common diseases is virtually the same as in the general population.

The proposed legislation defines family members to include distant relatives and adopted children (which have no blood relationship and therefore would not be affected by genetic information in the family). Proponents believed that the inclusion of individuals that have no blood relation (i.e., adoptive children) is necessary to insure that the family remains insurable as a unit; that adoptive children (or adoptive parents) are not penalized because one or the other has a genetic trait that they themselves could not have. Opponents argue that inclusion of distant or non-blood related individuals further extends the potential for litigation against insurers or employers.[7]

*Chapter 8*

# TITLE I. HEALTH INSURANCE

The bills propose protections against genetic discrimination by amending the Employee Retirement Income Security Act of 1974 (ERISA), the Public Health Service Act (PHSA), and Title XVIII of the Social Security Act (SSA) related to Medigap.[76] The bills do not contain one provision that was in S. 1053 (108th) amending the Internal Revenue Code of 1986. This provision would have covered health plans offered by church groups.

## MANDATORY TESTING PROHIBITED

Both bills would prohibit issuers of group and individual health insurance from requiring or requesting that individuals or their family members undergo a genetic test. Both explicitly state that the legislation would not limit the ability of a health care professional to provide health services even if they were employed by or affiliated with a group health plan or health insurance issuer. That is, health care professionals who are providing care may request or suggest that individuals or their family undergo a test.

## Prohibition of Discrimination in Group and Individual Market

Both bills would prohibit insurers in both the group and individual markets from using genetic information to determine eligibility or establish differential premiums based on the genetic information of individuals or their family members.

With regard to prohibition on genetic information as a condition of eligibility, the proposed amendments to Section 2753 of the PHSA would extend the prohibition to *include continued eligibility* of the individual to enroll in individual health insurance coverage.

## Privacy: Use of Information by Insurers

The bills contain a privacy and confidentiality section (Section 104) requiring coordination with HIPAA and HHS privacy regulations. The bills would assure coordination between HHS and the Department of Labor in implementing additional requirements pertaining to privacy, insurance and labor. Specifically, a group health plan, health insurance issuer or issuer of a Medicare supplemental policy would be prohibited from requesting, requiring, or purchasing genetic information for the purposes of underwriting, determining eligibility for enrollment (before or during the enrollment process), for premium rating, or for creating, renewing or replacing a health insurance contract. "Incidental collection" of genetic information would not be considered a violation, and the confidentiality standards would not apply to plans or insurance issuers that are not otherwise covered by HIPAA and the HHS privacy regulations.

## Enforcement

The bills would permit the Secretary to impose a penalty of \$100 per day during a period of noncompliance within the terms of Title I. Where willful neglect is found, they would establish a minimum penalty of \$2,500 or \$15,000 for more severe or prolonged violations.

If the proposed legislation becomes law, this title would take effect 18 months after the date of enactment of the act.

## Questions about Title I

In addition to the issues discussed above, the bills raised other questions and concerns, discussed below.

## Flow of Genetic Information in Health Care Operations

Certain stakeholders affected by the legislation proposed in the 108th suggested that bill language more clearly differentiate between information that is necessary for health care professionals (particularly those in group health plans) to carry out the functions and activities of the practice of medicine, and information that is necessary for the insurance issuer to carry out the functions and activities of administering the health plan. Others argue that those functions were explicitly separate (with underwriting housed within the health insurance issuer function), particularly for large insurers. One possibility would have been to clarify the conditions under which use of predictive genetic information would be prohibited (i.e., specifically for the purposes of underwriting). While both current bills have rules of construction which allow for the disclosure of information between health care professionals in the context of providing care, they contain no further stipulations regarding other uses of information. By contrast, H.R. 1910, introduced in the $108^{th}$ Congress, would have permitted disclosure of information to health plan employees for the purposes of paying claims or determining medical benefit so that those processes were not compromised.

## Privacy Provisions

Given the HIPAA privacy regulations, some have questioned whether additional privacy and confidentiality provisions are necessary. Others argue that while HIPAA addresses what to do with information that has already been obtained, the proposed bills would address more specifically the acquisition of information. HIPAA privacy protections are limited to the provision of medical services, and to the exchange of identifiable patient information during the context of health care operations, and do not extend outside of those operations to other groups (such as an employer that sponsors the health plan). The genetic nondiscrimination legislation would extend the privacy regulations to insurance and employment functions beyond those associated with the operation of a medical plan delivering health services. In other words, the bills would clarify the permitted uses of information as exchanged between plan sponsors (employers) and the group health plans.

## IMPACT ON UTILIZATION

Some individuals are concerned that the legislation, which is intended to increase utilization of health care services and participation in clinical studies, would actually reduce utilization because of the difficulty imposed by overly burdensome provision; for example, the requirement to keep genetic information in a separate file. A separate file requirement would be a provision in Title II (employment) (below). Thus, the requirement would not apply to groups covered by Title I (health insurers), even those that are sponsored by employers as employee benefit packages, and would not affect the use of services within the group health plan. HIPAA currently requires that confidential medical information be available only to those that need the information to do their jobs. This group would include the professionals who determine whether a genetic test or service is appropriate for an individual, and the administrators who determine medical benefit and payment. Arguably, the "separate file" concept is to maintain confidential medical information separate from confidential administrative information (such as the type that employers keep).

## MINIMUM PENALTY

Some have argued that the establishment of a minimum penalty would increase the incentive for individuals to sue health plans for violations of privacy or denial of coverage based on genetic information. Furthermore, some feel that establishing a minimum penalty in particular could act as a disincentive for settling disagreements. Others argue that the penalty clauses are equivalent to those in other civil rights legislation. They pointed out that appropriate penalties are necessary to deter discriminatory practice.

*Chapter 9*

# TITLE II. EMPLOYMENT

Both bills would cover the employers and employees as defined in Sections 701 and 717 of the Civil Rights Act of 1964, state employees and employers described in the Government Employee Rights Act of 1991, employees and employers described in the Congressional Accountability Act of 1995 and as defined in Section 3 U.S.C. 411(c), and job applicants.

## MANDATORY TESTING PROHIBITED

Both bills would prohibit employers, employment agencies and labor organizations from requiring or requesting that an individual or a family member undergo a genetic test. Both stipulate that nothing in them would limit the ability of a professional to provide health services; that is, health care professionals who are providing care may request or suggest that individuals or their family members undergo testing in the context of providing care.

## DISCRIMINATION IN EMPLOYMENT PRACTICES PROHIBITED

Both bills would prohibit discrimination by employers, employment agencies, and labor organizations against an employee or job applicant in making hiring or promotion decisions and in determining eligibility or selection for participation in training programs or apprenticeships on the basis of genetic information.

## Acquisition of Genetic Information by Employers

Generally, both bills would prohibit employers, employment agencies, and labor organizations from requesting, requiring or purchasing genetic information. They would allow employers, employment agencies and labor organizations) to acquire genetic information about an individual in the following circumstances:

- when they offer a health service program;
- when the employee provides written authorization;
- when the information is used to monitor the biological effects of toxic substances in the workplace, but only if:
  - the employer provides written notice of genetic monitoring;
  - the employee provides written authorization;
  - the genetic monitoring is required by federal or state law;
  - the employee is informed of the monitoring results;
  - the monitoring is conducted in compliance with federal genetic monitoring regulations; and
  - the identity of specific employees is not disclosed.

In addition, the proposed bills would allow an employer to obtain genetic information in the following situations:

- when the employer inadvertently requests or requires family medical history;
- when the employer offers health or genetic services, and the individual provides authorization;
- when the identity of specific employees is not disclosed;
- when the employer requests information to comply with Section 103 of the Family and Medical Leave Act;
- when the employer purchases publically available documents that may include family medical histories (books, magazines, etc).

## PRIVACY: USE OF GENETIC INFORMATION BY EMPLOYERS

Both bills would treat genetic information as part of the individual's confidential medical record, and require the employer to maintain separate forms or files for genetic information if they obtain it. Disclosure of information would be prohibited except when disclosure is:

- to the individual or employee at their request (including family members if family members are receiving services);
- to an occupational or other health researcher in compliance with 45 CFR Part 46;[77]
- in response to a court order when the employer has given the employee notice and sufficient time to challenge the order;
- to government officials investigating compliance with Title II.

Limitations on disclosure would apply to the employer, employment agency, labor organization and labor-management committee.

With regard to disclosure under a court order, the bills would limit disclosure to only the genetic information specifically authorized in the order, and would include an exception on disclosure made in connection to an employee's compliance with certification provisions of Section 103 of the Family and Medical Leave Act.

## ENFORCEMENT

Both specify that the proposed new legislation would not limit employees' rights or protections under the ADA or Rehabilitation Act of 1973 or any other federal or state statutes. Neither bill would have applied to the Armed Forces Repository of Specimen Samples for the Identification of Remains. Both would create penalties for violation of the non-discrimination legislation though the specific details differed.

The proposed legislation would establish a Commission to review the science of genetics and make recommendations on whether the "disparate impact" is necessary to continue to protect individuals from situations where an employer (with no discriminatory intent) unwittingly violates the law, and as a result, disproportionate adverse effects are experienced by some individuals with certain genetic information.

If the proposed legislation becomes law, this title will take effect 18 months after the date of enactment of the act. If the House bill became law, this title would have taken effect on October 1, 2005.

## QUESTIONS ABOUT TITLE II

In addition to the issues discussed above, the bills raised other questions and concerns, discussed below.

## THE GROUP HEALTH PLAN AND THE EMPLOYER

Some have argued that the legislation is not clear on how and when information could flow between the employer and the group health plan that is offered as a privilege of employment, and that the lack of clarity further confuses the HIPAA privacy issue. HIPAA protections apply to employee benefit plans with more than 50 participants when the plan provides medical care to employees or their dependents either directly or through insurance, regardless of whether they are insured or self-insured plans. The privacy rule includes group health plans, even those where the employer simply pays an insurer to administer benefits. It does not, however, regulate the employers who sponsor the group health plan (unless the employer is a health plan, or acts to provide on-site medical benefits). Thus, if health plans disclose health information to the plan sponsor, the information no longer would be protected by the privacy rule. As a result, the privacy regulations state that the group health plan portion of an employer may not disclose identifiable protected health information to the non-health plan portion of the employer without proper documentation and restrictions.[78] These protections do not apply to summary information or de-identified information.

In the past, opponents argued that genetic nondiscrimination bills, including the 108th's S. 1053 that is practically identical to S. 306 and H.R. 1227 in the 109th, did not adequately clarify the restrictions on disclosure of genetic information between functional units of the workplace (e.g., those that are providing employee welfare programs, such as cholesterol screening, and others such as the human resources department). Supporters indicated that the bills did not change the foundation of protections established by HIPAA and the privacy rule. Instead, the net affect of the proposed legislation would be to build upon that foundation, to clarify the role of genetic information in the context of other health information, and to establish specific protections for genetic information for entities that are not described by HIPAA (e.g, plan sponsors).

## Create Incentive for Litigation

Some argue that provisions to permit individuals to sue without first filing a complaint with the EEOC coupled with the absence of a cap on compensatory and punitive damages would only stimulate and encouraged litigation.[79] As with Title I, others indicate that penalties are both consistent with remedies under existing civil rights legislation (e.g., ADA) and are necessary to assure compliance with the provisions.

## Public vs. Individual Risk

Some argue that the bills are not clear about situations in which individuals have the right to put themselves at risk of harm or ill health, even if genetic test indicates possibility for illness with exposure, and when the employer would have the right to deny employment on the basis that the individual's genetic condition could place others in danger. Others state that it is unfair to deny healthy people opportunities when only a *possibility* of becoming ill exists. Even if it could be known that they would definitely become ill (as in the case with Huntington's Disease), *when* the illness would manifest to the point of preventing the employee from doing job remains uncertain. OSHA currently has guidelines for monitoring for genetic changes associated with exposure in the workplace and susceptibility to exposure (29 C.F.R. Part 1910).

## Sunset Clause

Some opponents argue that any genetic nondiscrimination legislation should have an expiration date to enable public policy to keep pace with scientific advances and allow Congress to decide how effectively the law has worked. This type of sunset clause is unprecedented in civil rights legislation; there is only one example of civil rights legislation that has an expiratory term.[80] Supporters of nondiscrimination legislation point out that Congress always reserves the right to evaluate the effectiveness of laws and make modifications as deemed necessary. Further, they do no believe that discrimination issues will go away in the near term. For example, a sunset provision may not protect a fetus, neonate or child tested today who would be seeking employment and insurance in the future.

## SEPARATE MEDICAL FILES

Some have argued that requiring maintenance of genetic information in separate files increases potential for medical error. Because the language states that the requirement applies only to *employers*, the risk of medical error would only increase if Title II could be construed to include group health plans administering employer-sponsored benefits. No federal or state law has a separate file requirement for group health plans acting to provide medical services, even though some studies show some physicians and genetic professionals are already keeping separate files in the absence of protecting legislation.[81] In fact, Executive Order 13145 (65 FR 6877) already requires federal agencies, acting as employers, to maintain genetic information as part of their "confidential medical records which must be kept apart from personnel files."

## SAFE HARBOR

Because states vary widely in their approaches to genetic nondiscrimination legislation, opponents of federal legislation propose that bills should include a "safe harbor" protection whereby employers that abide by the federal legislation are protected from violations of state or local law. The current bills propose a 'floor' for non-discrimination. This means that states with no discrimination provisions would have to meet federal standards; however, the federal law would not pre-empt more comprehensive state legislation.

# GLOSSARY OF TERMS AND ACRONYMS

**ADA** Americans with Disabilities Act (P.L.101-336)., 42 U.S.C. Section 12101 et seq.

**Allele** The specific version of a gene that is located on a chromosome. Normally, individuals will have two alleles for each gene, one located on each chromosome in a set.

**Amino acid** The building blocks of *protein*.

**Aneuploidy** Abnormal number *chromosomes*; a number of chromosomes other than 46 for humans. Examples: Down syndrome (47 chromosomes due to the extra chromosome 21), Turner syndrome (45 chromosomes due to a missing sex chromosome), or triploidy (69 chromosomes — a complete extra set of 23).

**Autosome** The 22 pairs of *chromosomes* that are the same in both males and females.

**Base** Nucleic acid building blocks of *DNA*. There are four different bases: adenine (A), thymine (T), guanine (G) and cytosine (C).

**Carrier** A person who has one *recessive gene* for a disease, condition or trait that is hidden by second *dominant* gene. A carrier usually does not show any signs of the disease, condition or trait. For example, a person who has cystic fibrosis has two copies of a disease-related gene. A person with only one copy of the disease gene would be a carrier of CF and would not show signs or symptoms of the disease.

**Chromosome** A long stretch of *DNA* that contains genes and other information. Humans have 46 chromosomes, which arrange during cell division in pairs of two (23 sets). During reproduction, each parent contributes one set of 23 chromosomes to their offspring.

**Chromosome abnormality** A chromosome abnormality can refer to an abnormal number of chromosomes (*aneupoloidy*) or abnormal structure (includes *translocations*). In a clinically evident chromosome abnormality, large pieces of the chromosome are typically lost or duplicated.

**CLIA** Clinical Laboratory Improvement Act (P.L. 100-578).

**Clinical sensitivity** The proportion of times a test result is positive when a disease, condition or trait is present.

**Clinical specificity** The proportion of times a test result is negative when a disease, condition, or trait is absent.

**Co-Dominant Different** (heterozygous) traits or alleles that are expressed (or are apparent) at the same time (i.e., blood type (AB)).

**DOE** United States Department of Energy.

**Dominant** A trait that is expressed or apparent when only one copy of the gene is present.

**DNA** Deoxyribonucleic acid; a large, double-stranded nucleic acid molecule arranged like a staircase (double helix); the chemical substance of which genes are composed.

**Enzyme** A special kind of *protein* that can cause biochemical reactions to occur.

**ERISA** Employment Retirement Income Security Act (P.L. 93-406).

**False negative** A test result that is negative when a disease, condition or trait is present.

**False positive** A test result that is positive when a disease, condition or trait is absent.

**Family history** A record of diseases, conditions, or traits in a nuclear (parents, children) or extended (grandparents, aunts, uncles, cousins, etc.) family.

**FDA** United States Food and Drug Administration.

**Gene** A stretch of DNA that carries information from one generation to the next and codes for a specific *protein.*

**Gene chip technology** A form of genetic analysis in which many hundreds or thousands of genes, parts of genes, or gene products can be analyzed simultaneously (see also *multiplex testing*). Gene chips typically have detection reagents (material that will pull out the gene, gene part, or gene product from a sample of interest) fixed to a solid surface, like a glass slide.

**Gene product** Heritable information carried by genes. A gene, composed of DNA, is transcribed into *RNA* which is translated into a *protein*. Both the RNA and protein are gene products.

**Genetic marker** A piece of *DNA, RNA, protein* or other genetic material that has an association with a disease, condition or trait (*phenotype*) of interest.

**Genetic variation** The variation in a population's *phenotype* (appearance) that is caused by differences in the *genotype* (specific genes). The DNA base sequence of human genes is about 99.9% identical among individuals. Approximately one of every 1,000 DNA bases varies among individuals, accounting for inherited differences in traits and disease susceptibility.

**Genome** The entire complement of genetic material in a cell; including genes and gene products.

**Genotype** The specific *alleles* (forms of genes) in a cell. For example, everyone has a gene(s) for eye color. The genotype would be the specific *alleles* that resulted in a particular *phenotype* like blue eyes.

**Haplotype** *Genes* that are close to each other on a *chromosome* so that they are usually inherited in a group.

**Heterozygous** When the *alleles* (forms of a gene) on both *chromosomes* (one inherited from mother, one from father) are different.

**HHS** United States Department of Health and Human Services.

**HIPAA** Health Insurance Portability and Accountability Act (P.L. 101-191).

**Homebrew test** A diagnostic test that a clinical laboratory makes itself. The laboratory produces the reagents, devises the testing procedure and validates the test to see that it works properly. By contrast, a *test kit* is made by a manufacturer. A kit is a combination of reagents and procedures that the manufacturer sells together in a convenient package for laboratories to use.

**Homozygous** When the *alleles* (forms of a gene) on both *chromosomes* (one inherited from mother, one inherited from father) are the same.

**Incomplete penetrance** The state that occurs when a person has a gene associated with a disease, condition or trait, but does not express the symptoms of the disease or condition nor has visible evidence of the trait.

**Karyotyping** A laboratory method in which cells in culture are grown to a certain point in their development. Cells are dropped onto a slide and "squashed", forcing the condensed chromosomes to spread out over the slide. Chromosomes are stained with a special dye and analyzed for shape, structure and number.

**Metabolic disorder** A disease or disorder of *metabolism*, the biochemical processes that occur in cells. Metabolic disorders usually result from the *mutation* of genes that tell the body to produce or not to a *protein*, or cause the *protein* to malfunction.

**Metabolite** Something that is needed for or produced by *metabolism* (the biochemical processes of cells). One example: drugs are taken to treat a condition. In the body, the drug is broken down (metabolized) into smaller molecules by proteins called *enzymes*. Both the drug (also known as a substrate), and the molecules are metabolites. These molecules can be measured to provide information about the efficiency of the process, which is in part determined by the proteins and by the genes that code for the proteins.

**Multiplex testing** Testing for many *genetic markers* at the same time. One example, would be *gene chip technology*.

**Mutation** In contrast to a chromosome abnormality, a mutation is an individual change in a DNA sequence that accounts for genetic variations. Mutations may be harmful if they prevent genes from making normal gene products. These mutations can cause, or increase susceptibility to, specific diseases or conditions. A mutation can be inherited from a person's parents, or acquired from exposure to a toxic environmental condition.

**Pharmacogenetic** Variations that are inherited in a person's DNA that are associated with how that individual's body reacts to drugs. Studies in pharmacogenetics generally look for markers that will predict whether an individual will have an adverse reaction to a drug, but can also investigate other aspects of drug metabolism.

**Pharmacogenomic** The entire complement of gene products that are expressed in association with an individual's reaction to specific drugs. Studies in pharmacogenomics investigate many aspects of the drug metabolism process; and many focus on identifying patterns of gene product expression that change in response to drug treatment, and whether those changes indicate that the drug is working.

**Phenotype** Observable characteristics (appearance) of an individual that are determined by the interaction of *genes, gene products* and the environment. Phenotypic testing identifies *genetic variation* by looking at the structure or function of a gene products rather than looking directly at the gene.

**PHSA** Public Health Security Act (P.L. 78-410).

**Positive predictive value** The proportion of times an individual has (or gets) a disease, condition or trait, given that he or she had a positive test result.

**Preimplantation diagnosis** A testing procedure performed on human eggs, sperm or embryos before implantation in the uterus to determine whether or not certain genetic disease, conditions, or traits are present.

**Prenatal diagnosis** A testing procedure done on cells that are shed from a developing fetus, usually between the third and fourth month of pregnancy, to determine if the fetus has a genetic disease, condition or trait.

**Protein** A string of amino acids that form a three-dimensional structure to carry out the functions of a cell. Proteins can be structural (give the cell shape), regulatory (act to turn genes "on or off"), or enzymatic (cause biochemical reactions to occur).

**Predictive genetic information** A *genetic marker* (or test) that determines whether or not a person will develop a disease, condition, or trait sometime in the future.

**Recessive disorder** A disorder that does not manifest (exhibit symptoms) unless both copies of a gene (*allele*) have a *mutation*.

**RNA** Ribonucleic acid; a single stranded nucleic acid molecule that carries genetic information from *DNA* to build a *protein*.

**SACGT** Secretary's Advisory Committee on Genetic Testing (Advisory Committee to the U.S. Department of Health and Human Services).

**Sex chromosome** Chromosomes that determine gender; females have two X chromosomes, males have an X and a Y.

**Single gene disorder** Relatively rare diseases that result from an abnormality in one *gene*, which usually alters the structure or function of a *protein*. The abnormality can be a mutation that changes the sequence of the DNA, an inversion (genetic material flipped around in reverse order), a deletion (loss of genetic material), or an insertion (addition of genetic material). Examples of single-gene diseases caused by each type of abnormality respectively are: sickle cell disease, hemophilia A, Duchenne muscular dystrophy, and some forms of Tay Sachs disease.

**Susceptibility** A possibility of disease caused or influenced by a *genotype*. Most diseases result from a complex set of both genetic and environmental causes. Some harmful gene mutations increase the likelihood that a person will develop a specific disease.

**Transcription** The process by which a *DNA* sequence is converted to *RNA*.

**Translation** The process by which *RNA* is decoded to produce a *protein*.

**Translocation** Rearrangement of a *chromosome*, which occurs during cell division, in which a piece of one chromosome breaks off. If the piece is lost, the translocation is unbalanced. If the piece combines with a different chromosome, the translocation is balanced (because no genetic material is lost).

**Variable expressivity** The possible range of symptoms or characteristics (extremely mild to very severe) that can occur due to the presence or absence of a gene. At this time, geneticists cannot predict the severity of many illness simply by looking at genetic markers.

**Variation** See *genetic variation*.

# INDEX

## A

access, 8, 25, 35
accounting, 57
accuracy, 12
acid, 8, 55, 56, 60
adenine, 7, 55
administrators, 48
adults, 36
adverse event, 22
advocacy, 29
affect, 3, 9, 13, 20, 48, 52
age, 11, 15, 19, 41
agent, 20
aggressive behavior, 4
AIDS, 22
alcohol, 21, 32
alcohol consumption, 32
alkylation, 32
allele, 9
alters, 60
amendments, 46
Americans with Disabilities Act, 17, 29, 55
amino acids, 7, 8, 60
anemia, 10, 30
animals, 32
anxiety, 22
asbestos, 31
association, 10, 57, 59
asymptomatic, 16, 27
attitudes, 21
availability, 11, 23

## B

banking, 25
banks, 27
behavior, 21, 30, 33, 35
behavioral genetics, 30
benign, 25
binding, 7
biological systems, 4
birth, 36
bleeding, 28
blood, 10, 19, 27, 30, 44, 56
body, 7, 19, 58, 59
bone marrow, 28
brain, 32
breast cancer, 16, 21, 28, 33, 34, 40
building blocks, 7, 55

## C

cancer, 9, 11, 21, 23, 28, 32, 34, 35, 36, 43
carrier, 55
cell, 6, 7, 10, 30, 56, 57, 60, 61
CF gene, 11
chemotherapy, 20

childhood, 32
children, 23, 28, 29, 34, 36, 44, 57
cholesterol, 20, 52
chromosome, 6, 9, 55, 56, 58, 59, 60, 61
chronic illness, 16
civil rights, 1, 48, 53
clinical diagnosis, 11, 30
coding, 7
cohort, 35
colon, 16, 21, 34
colon cancer, 16
community, 21, 28
complement, 6, 57, 59
complexity, 12
compliance, 50, 51, 53
components, 9
composition, 8
conception, 13
confidence, 10
confidentiality, 34, 35, 46, 47
consent, 23, 31
construction, 47
consumers, 16, 30, 33
context, 47, 49, 53
control, 9, 31
costs, 15, 16
counsel, 31
counseling, 34, 35
coverage, 28, 29, 35, 37, 46, 48
culture, 58
cystic fibrosis, 3, 10, 21, 55
cytosine, 7, 55

## D

damage, 31, 32
danger, 53
death, 13, 16
decisions, 2, 3, 17, 27, 35, 39, 49
definition, 2, 19, 30, 38, 39, 40, 43
delivery, 22
denial, 37, 48
deoxyribonucleic acid, 7
Department of Energy, 4
Department of Health and Human Services, 4, 58, 60
detection, 4, 11, 57
diet, 20
differential treatment, 11
disabilities, 38
disability, 3, 16, 17, 29, 37, 38
disclosure, 37, 38, 47, 51, 52
discrimination, vii, viii, 1, 2, 19, 21, 24, 25, 27, 28, 29, 33, 34, 35, 37, 38, 40, 45, 49, 51, 54
disease gene, 56
disease progression, 23
disorder, 11, 21, 23, 28, 30, 39, 40, 41, 58, 60
division, 6, 56, 61
DNA, 7, 8, 9, 19, 20, 23, 30, 32, 34, 40, 41, 42, 43, 55, 56, 57, 59, 60, 61
double helix, 56
Down syndrome, 3, 55
drug metabolism, 59
drug treatment, 59
drugs, 43, 59
duration, 32

## E

economic incentives, 23
employees, 16, 29, 30, 31, 32, 47, 49, 50, 52
employment, vii, 1, 2, 16, 27, 29, 31, 32, 34, 37, 39, 40, 48, 49, 50, 51, 52, 53, 54
enrollment, 1, 46
environment, 4, 20, 30, 59
environmental factors, 23, 32
enzymes, 59
equity, 25
ethnicity, 11, 24
ethylene, 32
ethylene oxide, 32

evidence, viii, 2, 13, 24, 27, 32, 35, 58
examinations, 16, 29
exclusion, 42
expenditures, 16
exposure, 20, 31, 32, 53, 59
expression, 59
expressivity, 61

## F

false negative, 10
false positive, 10
family, viii, 1, 2, 11, 15, 16, 19, 20, 21, 23, 27, 28, 30, 32, 33, 34, 35, 38, 39, 41, 44, 45, 46, 49, 50, 51, 57
family history, 11, 15, 21, 28, 29, 30, 34, 38, 39
family income, 35
family members, 20, 23, 39, 41, 44, 45, 46, 49, 51
FDA, 12, 13, 57
fear, 16, 21, 24, 33, 34, 35, 36
feedback, 33
females, 5, 55, 60
fetus, 54, 60
financial stability, 15
firms, 29
fitness, 29
flexibility, 12
friends, 34
funding, 4

## G

gender, 60
gene, 3, 7, 9, 10, 11, 19, 20, 22, 29, 34, 55, 56, 57, 58, 59, 60, 61
generation, 57
genes, 4, 7, 9, 19, 20, 22, 24, 30, 34, 38, 44, 56, 57, 58, 59, 60
genetic disease, viii, 10, 60
genetic disorders, 3
genetic factors, 24
genetic information, viii, 1, 2, 3, 7, 16, 19, 21, 22, 23, 24, 25, 27, 33, 36, 37, 38, 39, 43, 44, 46, 47, 48, 50, 51, 52, 54, 60
genetic marker, 2, 10, 11, 20, 21, 23, 25, 29, 31, 59, 60, 61
genetic screening, 17, 31
genetic testing, vii, viii, 3, 23, 24, 29, 30, 31, 33, 34, 35, 36
genetic traits, 44
genetics, 4, 5, 17, 37, 51
genome, 9
genotype, 9, 19, 57, 61
glucose, 24
government, viii, 35, 51
groups, vii, 2, 15, 24, 30, 33, 38, 45, 47, 48
guanine, 7, 55
guidelines, 53

## H

harm, 17, 53
harmful effects, 38
hazards, 30, 31
health, vii, viii, 1, 2, 3, 4, 13, 15, 16, 17, 19, 20, 21, 22, 23, 24, 25, 27, 28, 29, 30, 31, 33, 34, 35, 36, 37, 39, 40, 41, 43, 45, 46, 47, 48, 49, 50, 51, 52, 53, 54
health care, 16, 22, 23, 27, 28, 41, 45, 47, 48, 49
health care professionals, 45, 47, 49
health effects, 31
health information, viii, 2, 15, 16, 17, 22, 37, 52, 53
health insurance, vii, viii, 1, 15, 27, 28, 29, 34, 39, 40, 45, 46, 47
health services, 2, 45, 48, 49
health status, 4, 17, 19, 35, 40
heart disease, 3, 9, 22, 23
hemochromatosis, 34

hemoglobin, 10, 32
hemophilia, 28, 61
heredity, 24
hiring, 30, 49
HIV, 21
host, 20
human development, 5, 23
human genome, viii
human resources, 52
hunting, 32

## I

identity, 50
incentives, vii
incidence, 32
inclusion, 44
income, 35
indicators, 22
industry, vii, 2, 12, 33
influence, 23, 24
informed consent, 23
inheritance, 9
inhibition, 7
injury, 31
insertion, 61
instability, 30
institutions, 27
insurance, 1, 2, 3, 15, 16, 24, 27, 28, 29, 34, 35, 36, 38, 39, 45, 46, 47, 48, 52, 54
intelligence, 4, 24, 30
intent, 51
interaction, 4, 30, 59
interest, 5, 10, 25, 57
intervention, 11, 22, 23
interview, 35
inversion, 60

## J

jobs, 48

## K

karyotype, 6
karyotyping, 5, 6
knowledge, 31

## L

labor, 2, 46, 49, 50, 51
language, 47, 54
law enforcement, 23
laws, vii, viii, 1, 2, 15, 21, 35, 37, 38, 54
lawyers, 33
lead, 22, 24, 32, 34
legal protection, 35
legislation, vii, viii, 1, 2, 17, 22, 27, 37, 38, 40, 44, 45, 46, 47, 48, 51, 52, 53, 54
leukemia, 6, 32
liability, iv
lifespan, 19
lifestyle, 38
likelihood, 6, 16, 42, 43, 61
litigation, vii, 44, 53

## M

magazines, 50
males, 5, 55, 60
management, 10, 51
management committee, 51
manufacturing, 29
market, 12, 37
markets, 46
measures, 10
Medicaid, 12, 35
Medicare, 12, 46
medication, 20
mental health, 21
mental retardation, 3, 24
metabolic disorder, 3
metabolism, 24, 58, 59

metabolites, 9, 30, 40, 41, 59
military, 27
missions, 4
molecules, 59
monitoring, 31, 50, 53
morbidity, 6
mortality, 16
motion, 31
mutation, 8, 9, 11, 16, 20, 28, 32, 58, 59, 60

## N

national origin, 37
needs, 12
neglect, 46
nucleic acid, 56, 60
nucleus, 5

## O

obesity, 4, 22
organization, 29, 51
organizations, 33, 49, 50
ovarian cancer, 11

## P

parents, 44, 57, 59
penalties, 48, 51, 53
penetrance, 10, 58
perceptions, 24
permit, 46, 53
personal history, 32
personal responsibility, 22
pharmacogenetics, 59
phenotype, 9, 57, 58
planning, 33
plants, 5
polymerase, 7, 8
population, 11, 12, 44
power, 16
pregnancy, 22, 31, 36, 60
premature death, 16
premiums, 1, 15, 16, 29, 39, 46
preparation, iv
privacy, vii, 1, 21, 22, 23, 25, 34, 36, 37, 46, 47, 48, 52
production, 4, 7
productivity, 28, 30
prognosis, 30
program, 4, 31, 50
prophylactic, 28
proteins, 7, 9, 41, 43, 59
public administration, 29
public health, viii, 25
public policy, 53

## Q

quality assurance, 12
quality control, 12

## R

race, 24, 37
range, 19, 33, 61
reading, 8
reagents, 12, 57, 58
recurrence, 42, 43
regulation, 2, 12
regulations, viii, 37, 46, 47, 50, 52
relationship, 16, 44
relatives, 21, 23, 44
religion, 37
replication, 6
reproduction, 3, 56
reserves, 54
resistance, 42
resolution, 24
responsibility, iv
retrieval, iv
rheumatoid arthritis, 3
ribosome, 7
rights, iv, 24, 51, 53

risk, 2, 3, 9, 11, 12, 15, 16, 17, 19, 21, 22, 23, 24, 28, 30, 34, 35, 44, 53, 54
RNA, 7, 8, 9, 20, 30, 40, 41, 57, 60, 61

## S

sample, 57
saturated fat, 20
school, 27
scientific progress, 25
self, 7, 28, 34, 52
Senate, vii, 1, 22, 29
sensitivity, 10, 56
sequencing, 34
serum, 10
services, iv, vii, 12, 35, 47, 48, 50, 51, 54
severity, 16, 61
sex chromosome, 5, 30, 55
shape, 5, 7, 58, 60
sharing, 19, 23, 44
siblings, 23
sickle cell, 10, 21, 30, 31, 61
sickle cell anemia, 10
sister chromatid exchange, 32
sites, 7
skills, 30
smoking, 32
solvency, 16
specificity, 10, 56
sperm, 32, 60
stability, 20, 21
stakeholders, 47
standards, 25, 46, 54
statutes, 51
stigma, 20
storage, 23
stress, 39
students, 33
substance abuse, 30
substance use, 30
substitutes, 8
Supreme Court, 29
susceptibility, 3, 4, 7, 10, 20, 23, 30, 34, 40, 53, 57, 59
symptoms, 9, 16, 19, 22, 29, 56, 58, 60, 61
syndrome, 31, 55
synthesis, 32

## T

technology, 11, 22, 57, 59
telephone, 35
therapy, 42, 43
thymine, 7, 55
time, 1, 8, 9, 11, 13, 16, 22, 30, 33, 34, 40, 51, 56, 59, 61
tissue, 13, 20, 23
toxic substances, 50
training, 12, 41, 50
training programs, 50
traits, 4, 9, 19, 21, 23, 37, 39, 56, 57, 60
transcription, 7
transfer RNA, 7
translation, 7
translocation, 61
transplantation, 28
tumor, 20, 42, 43
tumors, 43
turnover, 15

## U

United States, vii, 3, 4, 56, 57, 58
urine, 19
uterus, 60

## V

variability, 43
variable, 6, 10
variable expressivity, 10
variation, 9, 10, 57, 59

victims, 23

## W

wages, 28
war, 23
warrants, 21
welfare, 28, 52
words, 48
work, 4, 10, 12, 22, 32
workers, 2
workplace, 17, 29, 30, 31, 50, 52, 53

## X

X chromosome, 60